now i lay me down to rest...

a peaceful bedtime prayer

by kimberly innecken

© 2014 kimberly innecken

all rights reserved. this book or any portion thereof may not be reproduced or used in any manner whatsoever without the express written permission of the publisher except for the use of brief quotations in a book review.

paperback isbn: 978-1-7368327-2-1
hardback isbn: 978-1-7368327-0-7
library of congress control number: 2021905669

book design by: jennifer vasko • 26point2designs.com

to treat all beings as my friend

my faith in love and life will be

what keeps me strong eternally

i love my family, friends, and me

it's love that keeps us all happy

...bless all my relations.

now my friend...tomorrow love eternally and love all

www.mjbpublishing.com

www.ingramcontent.com/pod-product-compliance
Lightning Source LLC
Chambersburg PA
CBHW042256100526
44589CB00002B/44